STEM BODY

THE SCIENCE of cancer

by Leah Kaminski

FAST READS

full tilt PRESS

The Science of Cancer
STEM Body

Full Tilt Press
42964 Osgood Road
Fremont, CA 94539
readfulltilt.com

Full Tilt Press publications may be purchased for educational, business, or sales promotional use.

Editorial Credits
Design and layout by Sara Radka
Edited by Renae Gilles
Copyedited by Nikki Ramsay

Image Credits
Flickr: SLAC National Accelerator Laboratory, 27 (top), U.S. Department of Energy, 10; Getty
Images: Brand X Pictures/Science Photo Library/Moredun Animal Health Ltd, 15, Brand
X Pictures/Science Photo Library/Moredun Animal Health Ltd, 28 (right), DigitalVision/
ER Productions Limited, 4, DigitalVision/ER Productions Limited, 18, E+/fotografixx, 12, E+/
Mark Kostich, 6, 28 (left), E+/Sean_Warren, 21 (top), E+/Willowpix, 20, E+/wilpunt, 27 (bottom),
Ethan Miller, 17, iStock/berya113, background, iStock/Dr_Microbe, cover, iStock/sanjeri, 29,
Time/Dimitrios Kambouris, 26 (bottom); Shutterstock: create jobs 51, 14, didesign021, 8,
Meletios Verras, 21 (bottom), nav, 23, sciencepics, 11; Wikimedia: Gerbil, 26 (top), National
Cancer Institute, 9 (bottom), Romina.cialdella, 9 (top), U.S. Department of Energy, 24

ISBN: 978-1-62920-838-1 (library binding)
ISBN: 978-1-62920-850-3 (ePub)

CONTENTS

INTRODUCTION

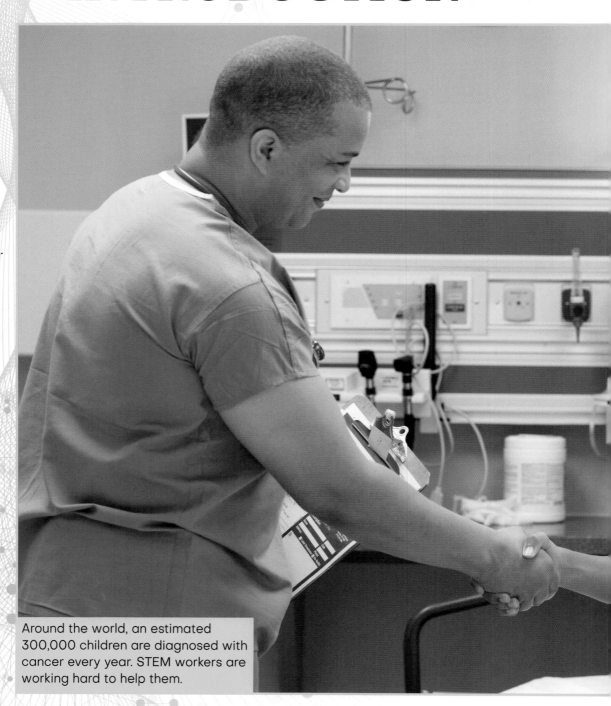

Around the world, an estimated 300,000 children are diagnosed with cancer every year. STEM workers are working hard to help them.

A young man is in a doctor's office. The doctor has just told him he is sick. He has been **diagnosed** with cancer. But both of them are smiling. They know that the cancer can be dealt with quickly and safely. The young man will need treatment. But he will be back to his normal life in no time.

That story could someday be a reality. People working in STEM fields are trying hard to cure cancer. STEM stands for science, technology, engineering, and mathematics. These workers are making treatments safer. Drugs are targeted directly where they need to go. New technology appears all the time. More people survive cancer than ever before. But progress is still needed. In the United States, more than 600,000 people die of cancer each year.

---

diagnose: to determine the specific illness or disease that is making someone sick

Zapping TUMORS

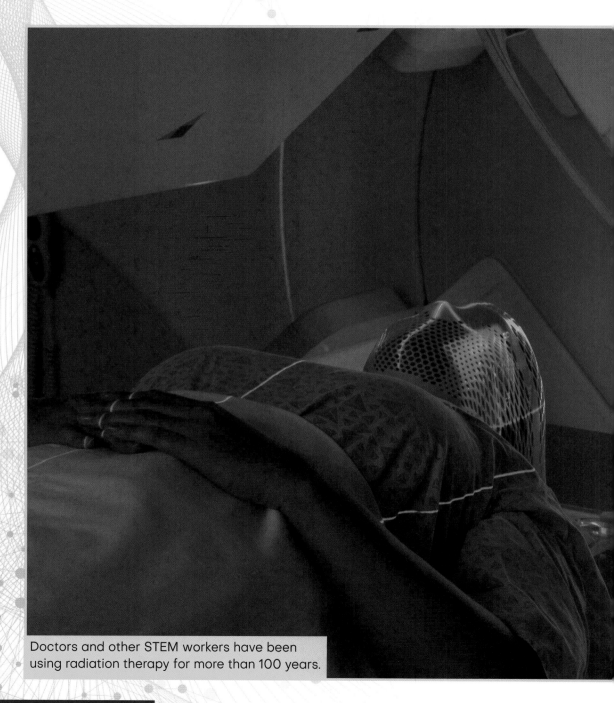

Doctors and other STEM workers have been using radiation therapy for more than 100 years.

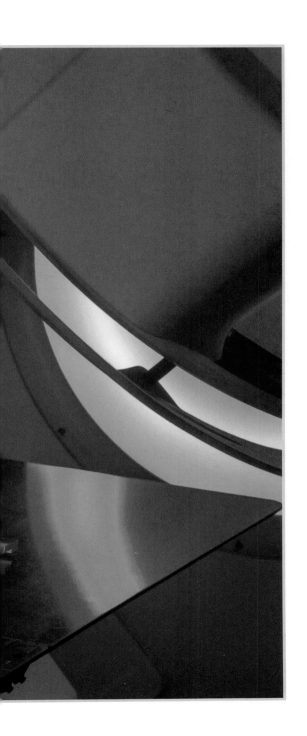

Radiation is a common way to treat cancer. In radiation, **electrons** fly through a tube called a **particle accelerator**. They speed up. They slam into metal at the end of the tube. This changes them into X-rays. The X-rays enter the body and kill the cells of a tumor. When doctors take X-ray images of a tooth or bone, very little radiation is used. For cancer, the amount is very high.

In radiation, the entire path of the X-ray beam affects the body. Healthy tissue is harmed. Also a patient's body moves when they breathe. Radiation hits healthy tissues that way too. Some scientists think that a faster dose of radiation would fix these problems.

electron: a very small particle that carries electrical energy

particle accelerator: a machine that causes charged particles to move at very high speeds and directs them into beams

Mice and rats are most often used in STEM research. Their basic biology is similar to that of humans.

Scientists at Stanford University are working on a system called PHASER. It works hundreds of times faster than radiation does. With PHASER, a flash of radiation is given. The flash lasts less than one second. This is faster than the body moves.

The research team is testing PHASER on mice. So far, tumors have been successfully killed. Side effects have been lessened. Now they need more powerful accelerators. The PHASER team is working on making the accelerator a different shape. Testing on humans is next.

French scientists are making something similar. It is called FLASH. FLASH doses are 1,000 to 10,000 times more intense than current radiation. They take less than 200 milliseconds. FLASH needs special machinery. But Swedish researchers have figured out how to use existing equipment for FLASH. As of 2019, FLASH may be ready for human testing in three to five years.

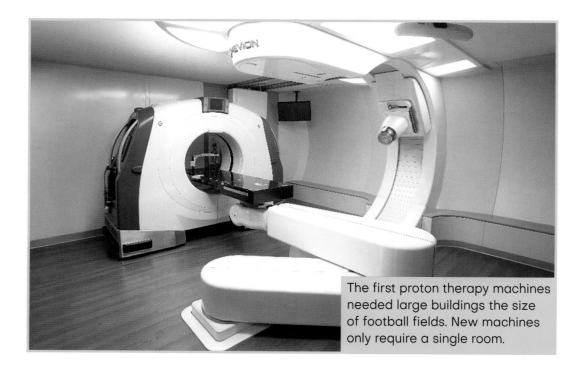

The first proton therapy machines needed large buildings the size of football fields. New machines only require a single room.

Proton therapy

In proton therapy, similar to radiation, tumors are blasted with beams of particles. But X-rays leave energy along the beam's path. A proton's energy is only used where it stops. This means that radiation does not affect healthy tissue. It only kills the tumor. Higher doses can be given safely. As of 2019, there were more than 60 particle centers operating and more than 60 additional centers planned. The therapy is promising but expensive. It requires magnets weighing hundreds of tons. The magnets slowly move around a patient's body.

RADIATION THERAPY

Radiation therapy is a life-saving and very complex form of medicine. To help zap tumors, workers from every STEM field come together.

SCIENCE
Research into X-rays led to radiation therapy. Many scientists worked on X-rays throughout the last century, including famous chemist Marie Curie.

TECHNOLOGY
To be safe, the equipment used for radiation therapy must be finely tuned. Mechanical engineers work on medical devices such as the gantry, which delivers the radiation.

ENGINEERING

CT scan technology uses computers to create a three-dimensional picture of a tumor. Computer engineers work on computers, including those used to make medical images.

MATH

Doctors must use math in order to decide on just the right dose of of potentially dangerous dangerous chemicals.

Precision MEDICINE

Geneticists are STEM scientists. They study how genes work, change, and are passed on from parents to children. Many geneticists focus on health and disease.

One way to understand cancer is to study **genes**. Cancer begins when a gene changes. The change allows cells to grow out of control. They can take over healthy parts of the body.

In the 1990s, scientists looked at every human gene. This was the Human Genome Project. Some genes provide instructions for building the body. There are about 25,000 of these in a human. Many diseases, from **Alzheimer's disease** to colon cancer, have been tied to specific genes.

Doctors can test people's genes. They can see if they have a high risk of getting some cancers. The genes of the cancer itself can be tested too. Doctors can see how the cancer works. Then they can treat it more directly.

gene: the part of a cell that influences how a living thing looks and grows

Alzheimer's disease: a brain disease that makes someone slowly lose their memory and mental abilities as they age

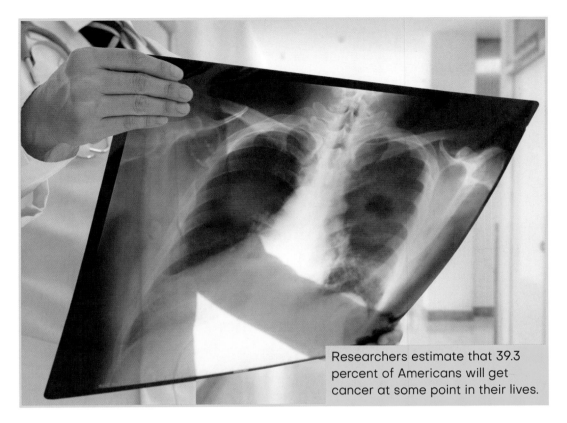

Researchers estimate that 39.3 percent of Americans will get cancer at some point in their lives.

Cancer used to be treated based on where it was. For example, all lung cancer was treated the same way. But tumors might act differently in different people, even if they're in the same body part. The same treatment for one person's lung cancer might not work for another. Too much treatment or the wrong treatment could be used. For example, chemotherapy kills cells all over the body. It might not be the right choice to treat certain cancers. Chemotherapy patients might lose their hair and get sick easily. The effects of chemotherapy may be very difficult for some patients.

Now doctors are learning to look at a cancer's genes instead of its location. Cancer cells are taken from the tumor. Doctors look closely at the genes. The cancer can then be targeted with treatments that have worked on similar cancers in the past. This is called genomic testing.

Common Types of Cancer, US 2019

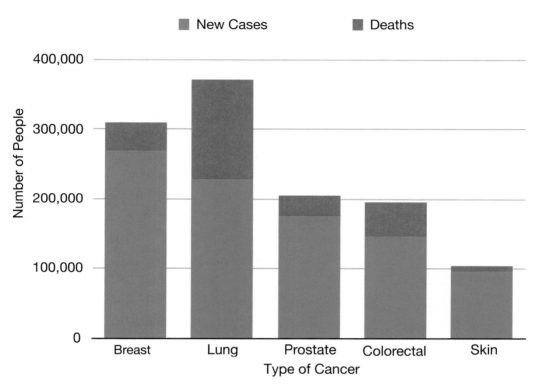

Legend:
- New Cases
- Deaths

Y-axis: Number of People (0, 100,000, 200,000, 300,000, 400,000)

X-axis: Type of Cancer (Breast, Lung, Prostate, Colorectal, Skin)

There are other new ways to attack cancer directly. One drug stops the cancer from growing new **blood vessels**. Tumors need new blood to survive. Doctors are also learning to target the cause of cancer. Some drugs block the changed genes that allow cancer cells to start growing.

blood vessel: a small tube that allows blood to flow to different parts of the body

Tumors are usually measured in centimeters. A 0.4-inch (1 centimeter) tumor is the size of a pea. A 2.4-inch (6-cm) tumor is the size of an egg.

DNA SEQUENCING

The first sequencing of the human genome was in the 1980s. It took 15 years and $3 billion. Modern DNA sequencers can read a person's genes in a day for $1,000. Many scientists, doctors, and engineers worked together to make this happen.

SCIENCE

The US Food and Drug Administration is behind an effort called BioCompute. This brings together many scientists from all over the country to make DNA sequencing science more reliable and easily shared.

TECHNOLOGY

The sequencer machine uses different kinds of technology to do its job. For one, it has sensors to analyze the light that reflects from different parts of DNA. Different kinds of engineers are behind each part of this equipment.

ENGINEERING

Computer software increased the speed and lowered the cost of DNA sequencing. Computer engineers write code and equations called algorithms to analyze data.

MATH

Behind the code used in DNA sequencers are researchers working in math and statistics. These mathematicians help solve the problems of how to analyze so much information.

Cutting-Edge TOOLS

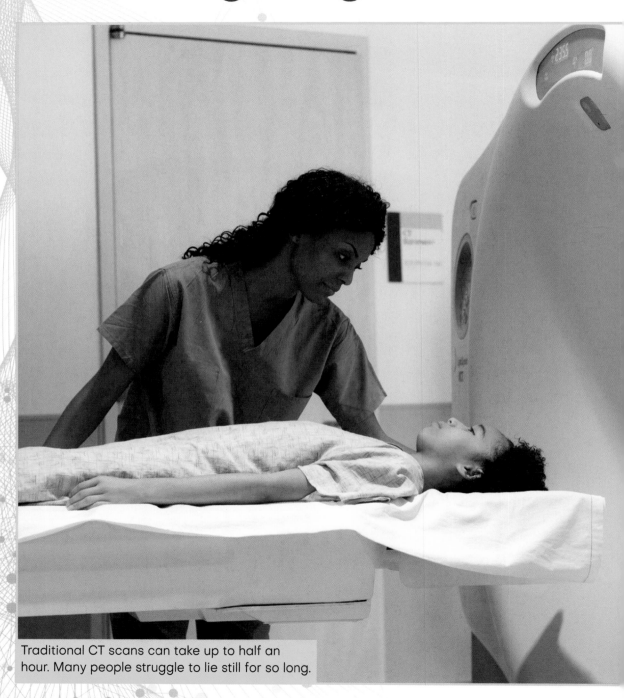

Traditional CT scans can take up to half an hour. Many people struggle to lie still for so long.

Doctors need to see the cancer inside the body. Using special machines, they find out where the cancer is. They find out its shape and size. This is called **imaging**. It helps them know where to direct radiation beams.

One special machine is an MRI. MRIs and accelerators were once used separately. First an MRI took a picture of the tumor. Then the patient got treated. Doctors couldn't see the tumor during treatment. They had to rely on the MRI from earlier. To make sure they hit the right spot, they often had to use more radiation.

A new machine has been made. It is called the MR-Linac. It uses an MRI machine and an accelerator together. It takes pictures of tumors at the same time as radiation beams hit.

CT scans use X-rays to take pictures of tumors. A new technology is called Proton CT. It uses protons instead of X-rays. Protons are better for the body. Scientists need to keep working on Proton CT. It needs to be much faster. That way patients don't have to stay still for so long.

---

imaging: a process that allows images to be taken and shown on a computer

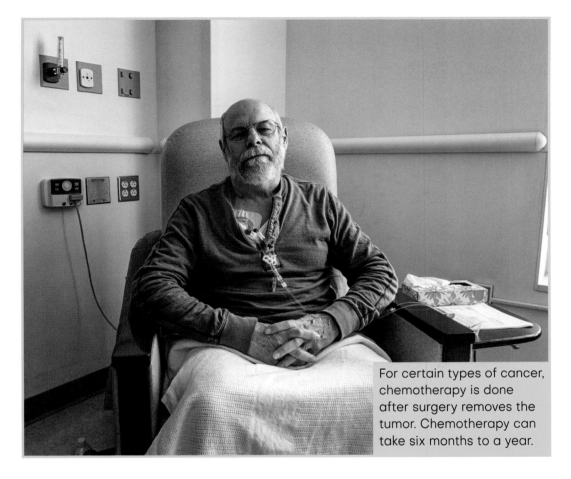

For certain types of cancer, chemotherapy is done after surgery removes the tumor. Chemotherapy can take six months to a year.

In nanotechnology, scientists design materials to be as tiny as **atoms**. New cancer treatments work like tiny machines. Scientists can control where, when, and how treatments work in the body.

There are many new nanotechnologies for cancer. One experiment is trying to treat brain tumors. A chemotherapy drug is attached to very tiny diamonds. The diamonds stay in the tumor longer than the chemotherapy drug would by itself. The drug can work better.

---

atom: a tiny building block of matter, invisible to the naked eye

Xiaoyun Chen's Nanovesicles

Dr. Xiaoyun "Shawn" Chen created tiny packages called "nanovesicles." The nanovesicles are injected into a vein. They travel throughout the body, including to the tumor. Chemotherapy is often injected into the body too. But unlike in chemotherapy, the nanovesicles don't affect the body until they get to the tumor. There heat breaks down the nanovesicles' shells. A cancer drug spills out and begins to work.

A company named Nanospectra makes a treatment called Auroshell. The tiny particles are made of glass. They are 20 times smaller than blood cells. The Auroshells are injected into the body. They are attracted to the tumor and gather there. A laser hits them and they absorb its light. Heat is produced, which kills the cancer cells.

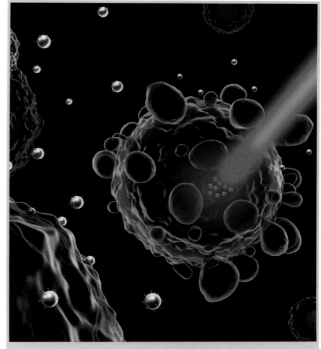

STEM researchers are also working with gold nanoparticles to create lasers small enough to only target cancer cells.

LINEAR ACCELERATOR

The MR-Linac uses two technologies to advance cancer treatment. The MRI makes images. The linear accelerator provides the radiation. STEM fields are behind both technologies.

SCIENCE

Scientists, not doctors, are behind linear accelerators. The ability to move and change electrons was a huge breakthrough in the 20th century. Science continues to move accelerator technology forward.

TECHNOLOGY

A difficult problem was solved in making the MR-Linac. MRI magnets could change the direction of the radiation beam. Scientists created a new technology where the MRI was split in half.

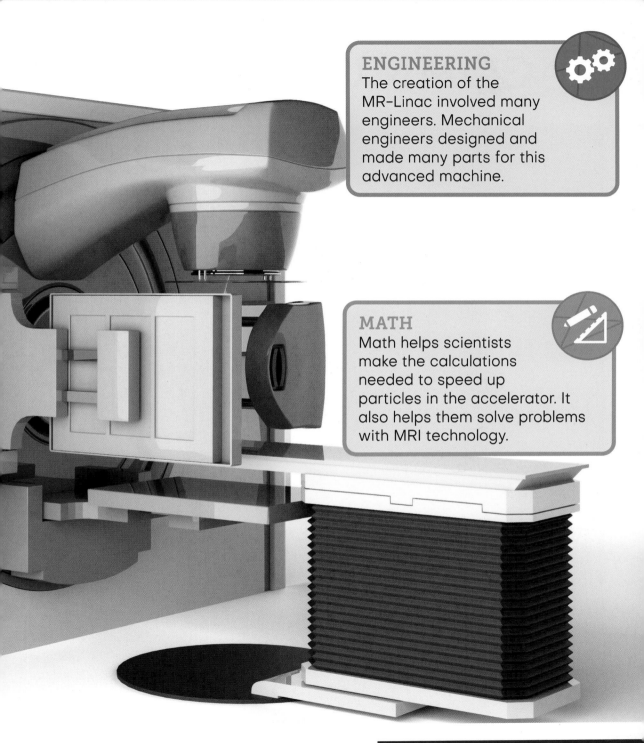

ENGINEERING

The creation of the MR–Linac involved many engineers. Mechanical engineers designed and made many parts for this advanced machine.

MATH

Math helps scientists make the calculations needed to speed up particles in the accelerator. It also helps them solve problems with MRI technology.

The Cancer-Curing COMMUNITY

Cancer researchers work for universities, government agencies, and independent organizations.

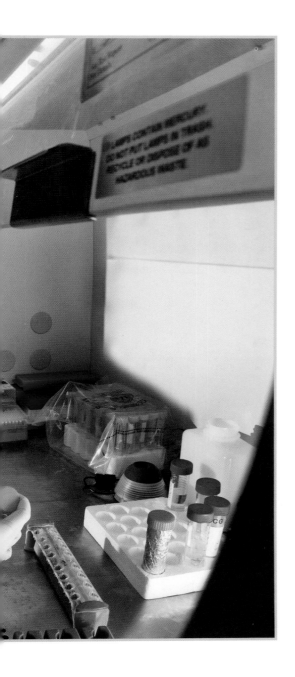

From the beginning, cancer researchers have been inspired by other scientists. Cancer doctors learn from **physicists**. **Pharmacists** learn from engineers. All of these are STEM fields. Each scientist studied science, technology, engineering, and math in school. Each ended up in a focused field. But they all work together.

Today the biggest advances are still made through teamwork. For example, the Department of Energy and the National Cancer Institute are two large organizations. They work together. The discoveries made by these scientists help many people. As more progress is made, it is possible that a cure for cancer will be found.

physicist: a scientist who studies physics (matter and energy)

pharmacist: someone whose job is to help prepare medicines that doctors prescribe for patients

CANCER SCIENTISTS

STEM workers from around the world are leading the way in cancer science.

CARL JUNE

June is a leader in cancer research. He was on *Time* magazine's list of the 100 most influential people in the world. He invented Car-T therapy. A patient's own cells are used to fight their cancer. June believes that not only does this therapy cure the cancer, but it will also protect the patient against that cancer for life.

EMILY WHITEHEAD

In 2012, Emily was a six-year-old with a dangerous form of cancer. She was the first child to receive Carl June's Car-T therapy. It worked. Emily is still cancer-free. She and her family started the Emily Whitehead Foundation. It helps raise money for experimental treatments for childhood cancer.

STANFORD LINEAR ACCELERATOR CENTER (SLAC)

SLAC is a world-famous research center in California. Scientists there are making accelerators. Accelerators are very important to radiation treatment. The first accelerator at SLAC was 2 miles (3.2 kilometers) long. Professor Richard Taylor was the leader of the team that made it. He shared the Nobel Prize for this work.

THE AFRICAN CANCER COALITION (ACC)

It is difficult to treat cancer in poor countries. The ACC believes that cancer treatments must not leave the poor behind. Sub-Saharan Africa is made up of 46 countries. More than 600,000 people get cancer there every year. The ACC helps these countries improve their cancer treatment.

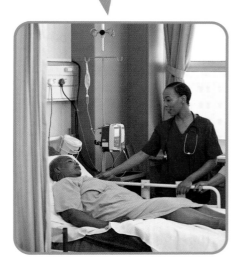

QUIZ

1 How many people die of cancer each year in the United States?

2 A PHASER flash of radiation lasts how long?

3 Which famous scientist worked on X-rays throughout the last century?

4 How many genes are in a human?

5 Researchers estimate what percent of Americans will get cancer?

6 What organization is behind BioCompute?

7 What type of STEM workers designed and made parts for the MR-Linac?

8 What did Carl June invent?

ACTIVITY

Imagine a New Cancer Treatment

Any cure for cancer will depend on scientific research and creative thinking. You can develop your own ideas to come up with a new type of treatment.

STEPS

1. Choose one of the most common cancer types. Read websites about this type of cancer. How is it diagnosed? How does it spread? Where in the body is it located?

2. Find out how it's treated. There are three common ways that doctors treat cancer. They are surgery, radiation, and chemotherapy. Which one is most commonly used for the cancer you've chosen? What are some of its side effects?

3. Plan a new treatment for the cancer. It can be surgical, drug based, or radiation based. Or see if you can come up with a completely new method. Does it use nanotechnology? A special surgical instrument? A new radiation setup?

4. Describe the treatment with a written proposal. It should explain how the treatment is created and how it works on cancer.

5. Draw a schematic of your treatment. An illustration can help you explain it to your classmates.

GLOSSARY

Alzheimer's disease: a brain disease that makes someone slowly lose their memory and mental abilities as they age

atom: a tiny building block of matter, invisible to the naked eye

blood vessel: a small tube that allows blood to flow to different parts of the body

diagnose: to determine the specific illness or disease that is making someone sick

electron: a very small particle that carries electrical energy

gene: the part of a cell that influences how a living thing looks and grows

imaging: a process that allows images to be taken and shown on a computer

particle accelerator: a machine that causes charged particles to move at very high speeds and directs them into beams

pharmacist: someone whose job is to help prepare medicines that doctors prescribe for patients

physicist: a scientist who studies physics (matter and energy)

READ MORE

Forest, Chris. *What You Need to Know about Cancer.* Focus on Health. North Mankato, MN: Capstone Press, 2016.

Honders, Christine. *What's It Really Like to Be a Doctor?* Jobs Kids Want. New York: PowerKids Press, 2020.

Marquardt, Meg. *Curing Cancer.* Science Frontiers. Mankato, MN: 12-Story Library, 2017.

Senker, Cath. *Science of Medical Technology: From Humble Syringes to Lifesaving Robots.* The Science of Engineering. New York: Franklin Watts, 2019.

Whiting, Jim. *The Human Genome.* Turning Points. Mankato, MN: Creative Education, 2019.

INTERNET SITES

https://thekidshouldseethis.com/post/how-to-design-a-particle-accelerator
Learn more about accelerators, including how to design one.

https://kidshealth.org/en/kids/cancer.html
KidsHealth explains the basics of cancer.

https://www.asco.org/research-guidelines/cancer-progress-timeline
Explore a timeline of the fight against cancer.

https://emilywhiteheadfoundation.org
Read more about the Emily Whitehead Foundation.

https://www.pbs.org/wgbh/nova/body/how-cancer-grows.html
Use an interactive site to learn how cancer grows.

INDEX